SAN FRANCISCO

PHOTOGRAPHY
AND
DESIGN
BERNARD HERMANN
TEXT
SCOTT BLAKEY
FOREWORD
DIANNE FEINSTEIN

les éditions du pacifique
papeete — tahiti

CONTENTS

FOREWORD

Bernard Hermann's brilliant photographs and Scott Blakey's sensitive prose combine to graphically show why San Francisco is the City most visitors to America want to visit.

San Francisco is unique among American cities. We are a diverse people, forty-two percent of whom are non-white. Strong ethnic and cultural heritages are seen and felt throughout many different neighborhoods of San Francisco. Fisherman's Wharf, Chinatown, North Beach, The Mission, and a score of other San Francisco neighborhoods reflect a long tradition of cultural openness and colorful life styles.

San Francisco is a city of contrasts. Steel and concrete skyscrapers in the downtown melt into colorfully painted and restored Victorian row houses in neighborhoods. San Franciscans passionately argue each new skyscraper, and neighborhood movements to halt their construction are strong. Problems of automobile congestion, increasing commuter traffic, freeways, and even the height and color of big buildings have been the subject of major public dialogue in the early Seventies in this beautiful City.

Out of these forums have emerged unique policies to control the height of tall building, buffer residential streets to prevent heavy traffic, and rehabilitate and renew neighborhoods. Cities without their families and children cannot survive, and one of the reasons that this book carries with it such a strong message of the flavor and spirit of San Francisco is that it also shows you our people.

We are a strong people, committed to our individualism and to the survival of this great City surrounded by bay and ocean. Of all American cities, San Francisco more closely lives the American Dream in her everyday life than any other city I know.

Dianne Feinstein.

SAN FRANCISCO

The San Francisco you see is a city of the '70's—the 1870's and the 1970's intermixed and interwoven, separate but equal, inseparable and unequal at once in harmony and at conflict with itself. Past and present co-exist in almost every neighborhood, in clothing, food, mores, architecture, lifestyle and transportation. It is boldly cosmopolitan and amazingly provincial, politically liberal and maddeningly reactionary. A lot of San Franciscans like it that way.

The city's attraction and mystique preceded the 1870's, of course, by 20 years and then some, but it did not truly blossom as a genuine cosmopolitan metropolis until it shook off the boom-town mentality fostered by the gold rush of 1849-1850.

Its naturel setting amid bay and hills, its peculiar qualities of light and weather, its grace and casual lifestyle, make it a desirable place to live. But there is something more, something inexplicable, that makes people stay here when they should have left long ago, and people migrate here when they should have stayed at home. Perhaps part of it is the knowledge that by living here, one belongs to a very exclusive family.

San Francisco is a small city; do not be deceived by photographs of it. It has only 45 square miles above water (and another 55 underwater). Nearly 700,000 people crowd onto its peninsula, which works out to something in excess of 15,000 persons per square mile. The size of the city and its population indicate two things: it is impossible not to know what is going on in another part of town, because you are only 20 minutes away from anywhere; and you had best know how to get on with your neighbors with 15,000 of them living in your mile. It makes for tolerance.

A small population means a solid front in times of general crisis. Now San Francisco is a melting pot city where nothing ever melted. Its diverse population offers a wide range of opinion and ideas, but in times of trouble, differences fade. These citizens are, after all, San Franciscans first.

Finally, visitors should not be put off by the chauvinism of the natives; San Franciscans delight in sharing their city with others. The only problem is, it takes a lifetime to discover all its virtues; only its vices are easily seen.

Restless and mighty, San Francisco Bay spreads two trillion gallons of salt water over 400 square miles. It regulates the weather above it and influences life about it. The bay provides food, transportation, inspiration and recreation, offers salt mine and sewer, supports commerce and supplies beauty. It is constant where the land is continually changing.

Once, long ago before they vanished, the Indians told their children this great inland sea had been created instantly. The earth rumbled and shook and the sky blackened. The coastal mountains parted. The salt sea poured through the breach flooding the lowlands and advanced into the sun-splashed central valley. The sea brought bounty: fish, oysters and generations of tiny, succulent shrimp.

Men of modern science hold a contrary theory of the bay's creation. They say the bay and the strait through which the sea finally poured, and the surrounding lands were carved and moulded in a long, often cataclysmic, geologic era that began more than 100 million years ago, when much of California lay unborn beneath vast primeval sea.

The Indians made it sound more poetic; the result is the same: the bay is a great, natural wonder. And there would be no San Francisco, as we know it, if there first had not been the bay.

Nor if the bay had not flowed inland through the Carquinez Strait to the valley and up the belly of the American River where in January, 1848, a carpenter named James Marshall found telltale flakes of gold in the race at Sutter's mill.

Nor if the gold fever had not spread around the world as fast as men could shout, horses gallop, ships sail and telegraphers' fingers tap out the joyous news.

Nor when the gold seekers, the argonauts, pouring through the Golden Gate on their way to the digs, disembarked at the village of San Francisco rather than at Oakland on the bay's eastern shore which was closer to the gold fields, or Stockton which was closer still or Sacramento which was virtually on top of them. Why?

It was San Francisco's lot: chance, fate. It really does not much matter "why?" anymore. San Francisco offered what no other city or country, save, perhaps, for the legendary Cathay, had ever offered men before: dreams, and hope. Dreams of gold and hopes of instant wealth. The word went forth: on the banks of a great harbor, a dream city full of gold and power; new life; no pasts; full of strong whisky and easy women, crystal chandeliers from Austria and china from Dresden, claret from France and silk-skinned ladies from Buenos Aires, acres of green gaming tables and bolts of broadcloth, all of it carted into the bay of bays by ships from all the corners of the globe.

Dreams and hopes and gritty reality and the power of gold propelled San Francisco from a rude outpost to one of the great, cosmopolitan cities of the world in less than 100 years. Bawdy, bloody, boozy, beautiful San Francisco: built by gold, fueled by silver and propelled ever-after by narcissism.

Early in the year 1776, a Spanish expeditionary force extending its weary empire's claims north from Mexico established a tiny outpost on the edge of a peninsula in Northern California. The Spanish named the site Yerba Buena (which translates loosely as "good pastures") and began construction of a small fort and a mission. Until the Spanish arrived, no European —with the questionable exception of the English freebooter, Francis Drake— had ever before set eyes on this land or the incredible inland sea which spread away from it. But neither the great natural beauty of the geography nor the tremendous economic and political potential of the bay and lands around it appears to have impressed the Spanish. They were shortsighted conquerors and inept administrators. Spain ruled California for 55 years, neither wisely nor well. In 1821, the Mexicans sent the Spanish packing and ruled the northern province alone for another generation. But Yerba Buena remained, as it had under Madrid, a lonely outpost abandoned and all but forgotten by provincial authorities.

Until the Spanish stumbled onto it, no vessel had navigated the Golden Gate. By 1832, it seemed to perplexed Mexican officials that every navigator on the high seas knew where to find that narrow strait. In truth, others coveted California: the English, relying on Drake's 1579 claim; the French; the Russians, seeking expanded trade; the Americans, always looking toward the next frontier. The Americans were the hungriest, the youngest and in a sense the closest. In pursuit of their Manifest Destiny a trickle of Yankee military scouting parties and civilian immigration began across the Great Plains and over the forbidding Western peaks into California. The trickle became a flood and outraged Mexican authorities were virtually powerless to halt it.

On June 14, 1846, a brash group of Yankee settlers with clandestine aid from the United States Army raided the village of Sonoma, about 40 miles north of Yerba Buena, seized the Mexican officials there and proclaimed the California Republic. It was a short-lived nation, but it signalled the beginnings of rebellion. Three weeks later, American troops landed at the provincial capital at Monterey. On July 11, 1846, U.S. Marines from the American sloop of war *Portsmouth* occupied Yerba Buena, raised the Stars and Stripes over the plaza, and retired with local supporters to one of the village cantinas to celebrate the victory.

Mexico and the United States went to war.

In January, 1847, with the war still on, Washington Bartlett, the chief American magistrate at Yerba Buena, issued a proclamation changing the village's name to San Francisco, after the bay. It was a generally unheralded event.

A year later, the sharp-eyed Marshall made his golden discovery, and eight days after that, Mexican and American diplomats signed the Treaty of Guadalupe Hidalgo ending hostilities and ceding California to the United States.

The conquest of the golden, sunny state was not without its dark side. The Spanish and the Mexicans had dispossessed, ruthlessly, the native California Indians of lands, liberty and life. The ultimate conquerors, the Americans, did likewise. By the end of the nineteenth century only one Indian would survive. All the rest were gone, dead or scattered. In those frenzied years few noted that between 150,000 and 300,000 persons, a whole civilization, had vanished, forgotten and unmourned.

Time to mourn and reflect on Indians was a luxury San Francisco would not allow itself.

There *was* no time.

By the end of 1849, the former outpost was a boom town numbering a population of 35,000 persons—and counting. The gold hunters poured through the Golden Gate and onto the shore as the salt seas had poured millions of years before.

The great bay and the sandy peninsula which for centuries had escaped the world's notice was now over-run.

The lures of gold and dreams and hopes were irrepressible. The harbor which once sheltered the lonely whaler or a brace of merchantmen was now a forest of masts and spars stepped into the hulls of hundreds of ships abandoned by passengers and crew alike for the gold fields.

The '49ers came from every nook and cranny of the earth, a motley, polyglot herd with a single purpose: strike it rich!

Many did.

Others found only misery. Some squandered fortunes in the gambling dens of San Francisco. Others simply disappeared. And still others lost their riches to a breed of miner who preferred his gold already panned and sacked, and whose tools of trade were a quick knife and a .44 revolver. Many San Franciscans became wealthy as camp followers: merchants, bankers, businessmen, prostitutes, innkeepers, shippers, importers, teamsters, gamblers, tailors, blacksmiths, all purveyors of goods to the men from the gold fields.

The legend and romance of San Francisco was born in those crowded years of the 1850's, a wild, wide open, riotous town, colorful, extravagant and so very rich, teeming with life and death and spontaneity. It was reputed to be the most infamous port in the world. On its planked sidewalks strode every imaginable type of human being, saint to sinner. Sections of the city, housing populations of foreign-born, were regularly set upon by brigands and thugs. The Barbary Coast quarter was beyond control: City officials would not or could not exercise authority. Finally, respectable citizens took the law into their own hands to halt the violence. They formed Committees of Vigilance. The Vigilantes, in 1851 and again in 1856 established reasonable law and order, hanging a few renegades to show they meant business. The rabble moved on. In its early times, San Francisco burned and was rebuilt six times.

Gradually, a permanent city rose out of the original jumble of rough planks and tents and Mexican adobes that marked San Francisco in 1849. In time it would evolve style, even grace. Streets were plotted; whole hills were levelled and the sands dumped into the bay, into the hulks, to create more land on which to build. Buildings of stone and iron and rosewood were filled with the benchmarks of civilization: assay offices, newspapers, banking houses, schools, tradesmen, theaters, restaurants, manufacturers, business offices and families.

As suddenly as it had emerged as a city, San Francisco also emerged as the financial and cultural capital of the West.

San Francisco's life is relatively short and its periods of calm nearly non-existent. In the early 1860's, its economy went into decline as the gold fields were nearly picked clean; and, miraculously, the treasures of the Comstock Lode and other silver mines were uncovered, precipitating a second era of lavish spending and shoring up of the sagging economy. Up went more theaters, more business buildings, more saloons, hotels, more homes, all presided over by nabobs who dwelled in huge baroque mansions of wood and glass on Russian and Nob Hills. San Francisco had fostered a new nobility: silver kings, railroad kings, merchant princes and some lesser dukes of the realm of wealth.

And when silver dwindled, farms and ranches in the north and central valleys came into full production and new fortunes were made. The remaining decades of the Nineteenth Century marched resolutely toward the Twentieth, each marked by its own, distinctive events: the bitter labor disputes and anti-Chinese outbursts of the 1880's, the Alaska gold rush and the popular Spanish-American war of the 90's, and finally, December 31, 1899, that marked a turn of year and a turn of century celebrated in the city's usual exuberant fashion. The new year would see the successful conclusion of the Spanish war and increasing economic prosperity. Then, on April 18, 1906, it all came tumbling down.

The earthquake and fire which began that April morning marked a major turning point in the city's history. The magnitude of the shock alone was great enough to class it with the world's historic cataclysms. Only a few other quakes have ever equalled it. Local poets with the traditional narcissistic outlook composed verses praising the beauty of San Francisco's ruins. More practical citizens began cleaning up the rubble and planning for the future. Nature's wrath had been awesome enough: at least 450 persons dead, more than 500 city blocks destroyed, water supplies contaminated and food in short supply; thousands homeless and destitute; damages estimated to exceed $350 million (probably more than $1 billion by today's standards). San Franciscans wasted little time in lamentation. A new city quickly rose on the site of the old. If there was now a subtle sobriety unexpectedly created by the disaster and the knowledge it could happen again, there was also the determination that San Francisco would live again. The joyous celebration of ife returned and the reign of the Queen of the West continued without further interruption. The middle years of the Nineteenth Century had established the reputation of San Francisco: the year 1906 established the reputation of the San Franciscans as a brave and hardy group in the face of great adversity.

The opening of the Panama Canal which stimulated trade and fattened the city's coffers was acknowledged in style by the elegant Panama Pacific International Exposition of 1915. Not even the widening war in Europe dimmed the joy of that fair.

The next two decades saw conflict become reality and peace an uncertainty, the fanciful 1920's for which San Francisco's life-style was so admirably suited and the dark depression days of the 30's, for which it was not. By 1939 with the world again arming for war, San Francisco had finished construction of its two legendary bridges and celebrated its industrial and commercial supremacy on the Pacific Coast with the Golden Gate International Exposition at Treasure Island.

As the earthquake had moved the city from childhood to reluctant adolescence, the Second World War and the post-war era shoved it into maturity. Between 1942 and 1945, San Francisco was the major mainland supply point for the struggle in the Pacific and its population skyrocketed, as did that of the surrounding Bay Area.

The city occupied the world stage in 1945 when the United Nations charter was drafted in the Opera House and again in 1951 with the signing of the Japanese Peace Treaty.

On the surface, it was still grand, magnificent, insouciant San Francisco but its innocence was gone. The war had finally done it and the wars to come in Korea and Indochina would assure it: pride in financial attractiveness was shaken as the traditional fine-grained architecture and undistinguished skyline disintegrated, replaced by ever-multiplying skyscrapers, blocked views and promises of more to come. Increased population and urban problems unheard of a decade before, strained the city's traditional tolerance. The port went into decline and taxes increased.

Still, it was the dream merchant. Innocence might be shattered, but reputation and certain amenities of the old style were intact: boozy, bawdy, beautiful San Francisco. The Beatniks came in the '50's and the Flower Children in the '60's, the towers kept climbing; San Franciscans accepted the challenge. The 1970's ushered in a period of rapid social and financial change and San Franciscans again proved hardy, courageous and innovative, tolerating the strange while defending their city against those who would rob it of its remaining allure.

The gold is gone, but they still come to San Francisco, those who dream those who hope: from China, from Latin America, from Europe; from failing marriages in New York and bottomed out jobs in Fall River, from political tyranny and economic hopelessness. They come to San Francisco that queer

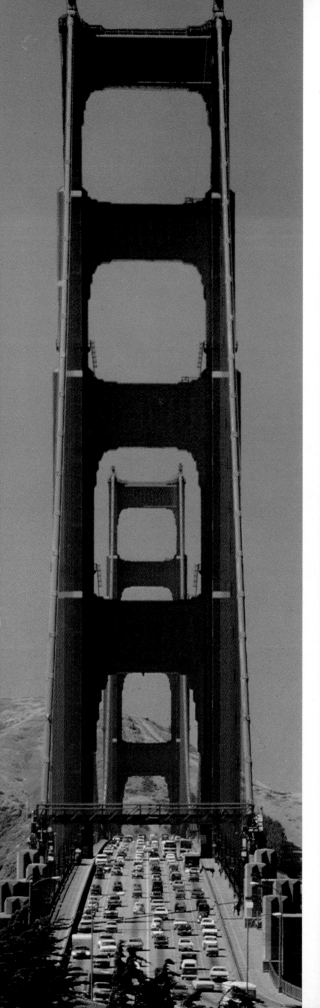

*It seems that John C. Fremont was
the first to coin the phrase "Golden Gate".
In his* Geographical Memoir of California, *1848,
he wrote: "To this Gate I gave the name
'Chrysophlae' or Golden Gate, for the same
reason the harbor of Byzantium was called
'Chrysoceras' or Golden Horn."*

San Francisco, small, compact, hilly, sits on the end of a small peninsula in Northern California. From its shoreline, north and east, spring two of the world's longest bridges, the Golden Gate Bridge, which is the city's symbol, and the San Francisco-Oakland Bay Bridge. On the western edge of the city is the Pacific Ocean; on its northern and eastern sides, San Francisco Bay, a great inland sea covering more than 400 square miles. Together, the city (with its distinctive skyline and hillside architecture), water, bridges and weather combine to make San Francisco one of the most unique and beautiful cities in the world.

For more than 100 years,
San Francisco's cable cars
have tamed the city's hills and
provided a most distinct
symbol. Above left, *a cable car
begins its long descent down
HydeStreet; Aquatic Park
and the Maritime Museum's
anchorage (the Hyde Street
Pier) are in the background.*
Below, *two cable cars meet
at the top of Lombard,
"the crookedest street in the
world."* Right, *the city's
traditional architecture played
against the downtown towers.*
Overleaf, *one of the city's
news vendors takes time out for
a smoke; mime Robert Shields
works in Union Square.*

This square was presented to the city in 1850 by Mayor
Geary, but only received its name in 1860 from the
pro-Union meetings held there. After the 1906
earthquake and fire, the square was used as a refuge,
mostly by the residents of the St. Francis Hotel.
Today it is the scene of all sorts of public
rallies, scheduled and impromptu, and a haven
for San Franciscans who come here and sit or
stroll amongst the pigeons. Several annual events
take place in Union Square, like the Rhododendron
Week and the Cable Car Bell Ringing Contest.

One trait of San Francisco's strength is its traditional tolerance and the diversity of its peoples and cultures, concentrated on a small and highly populated peninsula.

There is a thicket of towers that stand up around Montgomery Street in the heart of the financial district looking down their expensive noses at nothing in particular. To many people these buildings represent downtown San Francisco. They do not.

Downtown and the financial district are quite separate entities. The towers represent the financial district which, in turn, represents money. Downtown San Francisco can be a rather joyous place. The financial district is a serious place.

There is nothing droll about money if you are in the business of making it or increasing it or investing it. Money made San Francisco and San Francisco is hanging on as the financial mogul of the West. The money men built the towers to prove it.

The men who control Montgomery Street are keepers of the financial flame, heirs of men who weighed the gold and stacked the silver that built and fueled a city that was never grateful for them; while they counted, it caroused. In a sense the financiers built their own city; it is an empty place at night and on weekends while downtown San Francisco enjoys life.

The skyscrapers of the financial district, especially the whoppers that make for a unique—some say exciting—skyline, are of recent vintage. Most of them rose in the last decade. San Francisco traditionally built its buildings close to human scale.

In the earliest years, downtown centered around what is now Portsmouth Square in Chinatown. What is now Montgomery Street was the beach. They filled it during the gold rush to gain more land upon which to build and Montgomery Street was born. North of Portsmouth Square in the 1850's was an area called Sydney Town where the village hoodlums hung out. In the 1860's, it had become known as the Barbary Coast, an unsavory place favored by the renegades of six continents.

The counting houses around Portsmouth Square, and later Montgomery Street, earned San Francisco its financial reputation; the Barbary Coast provided the rest of the legend and all of the infamy.

One of the Coast's most fulsome (and profitable) enterprises was crimping, kidnaping sailors into literal servitude aboard ships which could not (or would not) hire regular crews. The process became known as Shanghaiing. The master of the art was Shanghai Kelly, a raw-boned yegg who worked out of a three-story building at 33 Pacific Street. When he received an order for "goods", he sent his lackeys into the streets with tales of free booze and free women to entice the unwary to his establishment. He never failed to deliver. The booze was always drugged. The ladies never materialized. The suckers never caught on. Stupid with drink, Kelly's goods were lowered through a trap door at the back of his joint and carted off to the waiting ships.

Kelly became, in 1875, however briefly, a local hero after he rescued the passengers and crew of a ship which foundered off Point Concepcion. Ironically, his heroics came as he was returning from his most remarkable feat: crimping in a single venture the crews for three ships.

(The crimpers were eventually put out of business by laws proposed by the Sailors Union of the Pacific, organized in 1891, and by writers such as Jack London who crusaded for decent jobs and rights for sailors.)

Changing times and San Francisco's increasing sophistication eventually tamed the Barbary Coast, though parts of it hung on until World War II. What was its central area is now called Jackson Square, tame but colorful. Antique shops have replaced the bawdy old saloons and crimpers' bars, decorators' boutiques the brothels and the cribs, gleaming galleries the gambling dens and opium joints. Many of the old buildings have been restored and among the shops and along the little alleys is a walker's paradise.

The Barbary Coast at its peak was larger than present-day Jackson Square, but not by much. San Francisco author Margot Patterson Doss once observed that visitors who walk the area today will not be surprised so much by the international infamy the Barbary Coast attained as by the small space in which it was attained—about six square blocks.

Contemporary downtown San Francisco covers much more than six blocks and its reputation is several cuts above that of its predecessors. Its attractions range from the Civic Center where the city's major government buildings are situated about a reflecting pool and tree-studded plaza to stately old hotels like the Saint Francis and Palace, the latter with its glass domed Garden Court. There is a variety of fine stores and shops and salons with gilt-edged names, galleries, elegant saloons and old, established businesses and tarnished areas, too, like the Tenderloin, with the tawdry and the troubled.

San Francisco's central boulevard, Market Street, has had a $24 million, voter-approved face lift; the new BART rapid transit system runs beneath it. Scattered throughout downtown and in some quiet corners of the financial district are an assortment of vest pocket parks and malls, filled with flowers and fountains and benches. There are other offerings: sculpture gardens, musical programs and art exhibits, all without charge. But in a city that dotes on mixing business with pleasure, past with present, there is nowhere it comes together better than a place called Union Square.

Union Square sits snugly on the bosom of downtown San Francisco like an antique cameo glowing on a dowager's breast.

One block long and one wide, it is the city's central forum. It is a place where San Franciscans can speak their minds or stare off into space, sit alone or congregate *en masse* or rest a while after a morning's shopping in the elegant stores of the neighborhood.

The centerpiece of this green little island is the soaring Dewey Memorial which is topped by a figure of Victory flaunting a never-wilting laurel wreath. The monument stands tribute to young America's trouncing of the rusty Spanish armada in the 1898 war.

For San Franciscans who take pride in the urbanity of their city and its tolerance, Union Square on any day is a showcase:

Two men with wrinkles of uncertain age converse in Italian syllables under wide-brimmed, stained fedoras and feed the pigeons stomping around their feet from crumpled paper sacks.

A young man in a tattered Army field jacket with a battered look about his eyes laments in reedy voice what he perceives to be the latest catastrophe to befall The People. His protest is unclear, but his denim-clad audience of three applauds in empathy.

A white-faced mime, dandied up in silver and black, apes with unerring eye a well-tailored, preoccupied businessman hurrying toward an appointment. The mime's admirers applaud while the subject of this mirth, suddenly aware, flees the impromptu stage with blushing grimace.

Rows of newspaper readers sit with backs to the sun. On the opposite benches, a geriatrics convention soaks up the heat, recharging old batteries for the shady afternoon.

Elegant women with expensive labels in their suits and gloves on their hands stroll through on their way to a long luncheon.

Scattered musicians strum and thump and blow a cacophony out of rhythm with the sharp ring-ading-da-ding-ding of the bells of the cable cars which click up and down Powell Street at the Square's western edge.

About the perimeter, street merchants and handicraft artists hawk their wares off make-shift counters, an activity that angers more conventional merchants whose tax-burdened goods and costly inventories reside on the shelves of more conventional stores that ring the square.

On an opposite corner an elderly woman supported by fragile ankles and faith, waves a well-worn Bible demanding repentance and future devotion to the Lord. Her fidgety audience is captive, trapped momentarily by a traffic light.

Peeking from behind a hedgerow, three gentlemen of the day dressed as ladies of the evening study the Bible-thumper slyly from under their wigs, then collapse in giggles. Repent? They have not yet begun to sin.

The pigeon corps takes wing only to resettle, cooing and flapping, moments later on the Dewey Memorial. Two little children below clap with delight. Their practical mother shoos them out of guano range.

Union Square was named sometime around 1861 after America's southern states had quit the Republic.

In the spring of that year, a great rally was held in the park bounded by Geary, Post, Powell and Stockton Streets. Speakers urged San Franciscans to cast their lot with Lincoln, and the Union. Thus they eventually voted. Thus the square was named.

The public still rallies there, for the wedding of the mime, to protest war or waste, to celebrate spring, to support striking airline workers, to marvel at opera star Beverly Sills in free concert, to exercise the right of free speech for anyone who cares to listen, to feed the pigeons.

It's traditional.

*There are almost 700,000 people
living in San Francisco itself, the center
of a metropolis of over 4.5 million inhabitants.
More than 50% of the population is of foreign
origin and newspapers are printed in 14
different languages.*

During the last two decades San Francisco's importance as a corporate and financial center has grown; so has its downtown skyline. With little land, but many offices and workers, there was no place to go but up, a situation which has upset city traditionalists who preferred the old, low-rise skyline. Pages 32-33, *San Francisco looking west from Yerba Buena Island and Bay Bridge;* pages 34-35, *a commuter's view of the city from the Bay Bridge* (left) *and the aging tower of the Ferry Building at the foot of Market street between two modern facades:* Left, *California Street drops from Nob Hill to the financial district;* right, *California and Montgomery Streets, the financial district.*

Indoors or outdoors, San Francisco offers treats for the eyes. Left, *one of the city's streetcorner florists;* below, *a mural on a Van Ness Avenue saloon.* Right, *the Garden Court at the Palace Hotel, and buildings old and new.*

When it comes to romance
and tradition, it is hard to
find a better example than San
Francisco's hardy little cable
cars, a local fixture since 1873.
Today's three operating lines
carry millions of passengers
over just 10 ½ miles of track.
When break-downs occur,
there is a wait in store for
would-be riders. In an age
of high-speed machines, some
persons find relief in the cable
car's steady nine miles per
hour pace, and well worth the
wait. Left and right,
waiting and riding on the
Powell Street line.

Street scenes: left, *news vendor on Market Street and an exchange of views between a patrolman and a doorman on Powell.* Right, *night fog blurs waiting cable cars at the Powell Street turntable.*

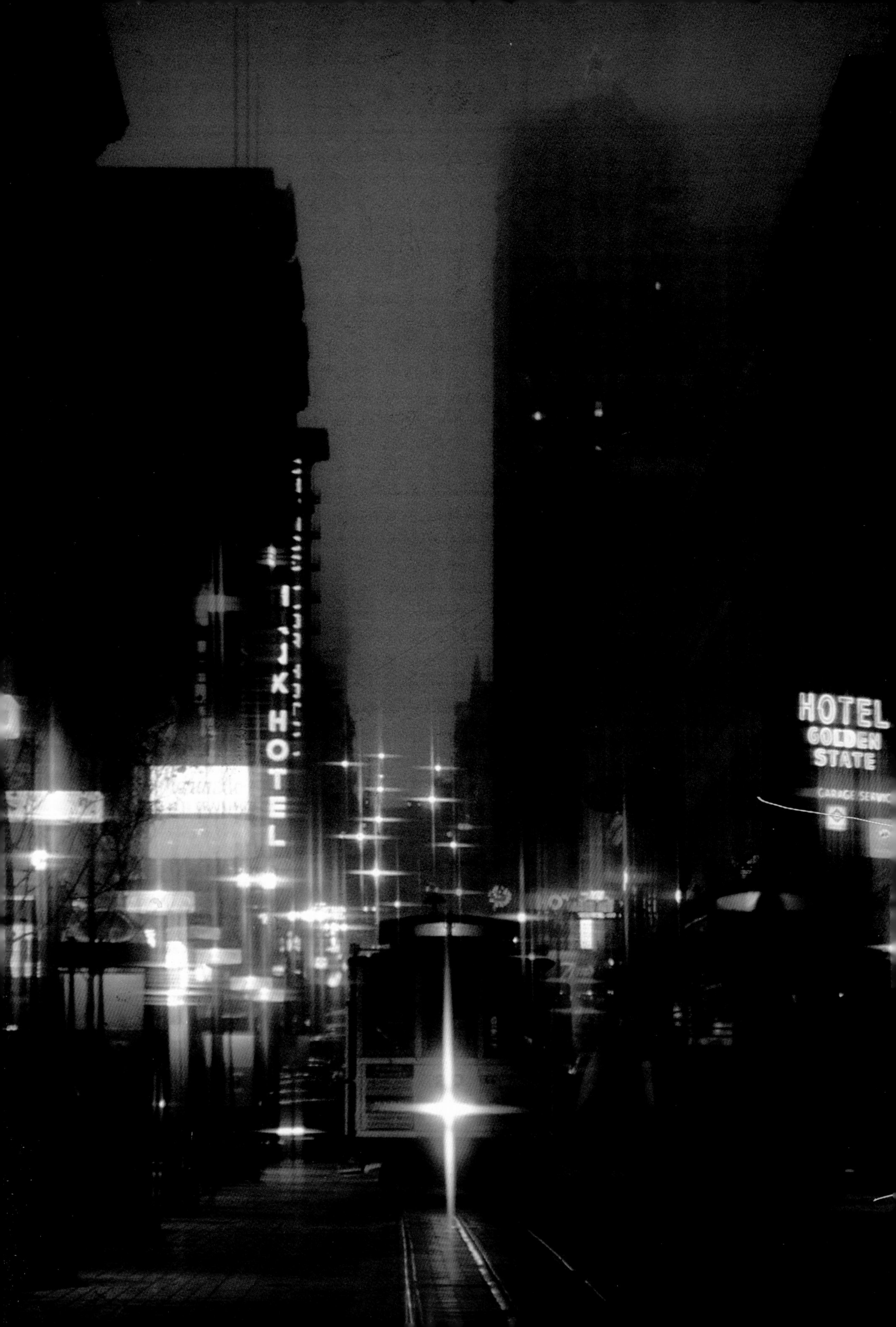
HOTEL
HOTEL
GOLDEN
STATE

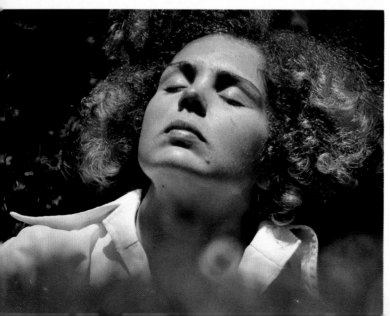

*San Franciscans have always taken advantage of the amenities offered by their city, including its parkland. Downtown, the park is Union Square with its trees and benches and daily parade of life. Pages 44-45, a cable car pauses on Powell Street at the Square's western end; the venerable Saint Francis Hotel is in the background.
Pages 46-47, Union Square provides excellent spots for sitting, sunbathing and daydreaming. Pages 48-49, there is very little one cannot see in Union Square. Its habitués tend to be blasé, even when faced with an occasional bizarre stroller.*

49

Some years back a writer observed that San Francisco valued the picturesque over the practical. His "picturesque" referred to the cable car; presumably "practical" meant the blessing of Twentieth Century technology. He meant no harm. He simply did not understand San Francisco and its views of traditional things and things traditional. Cable cars fall into the former category. Characters are examples of the latter. And Joshua Abraham Norton is a case in point.

He was an Englishman who emigrated first to Brazil where he was engaged in trade, and then to San Francisco where he stepped ashore in 1849 with a respectable bankroll. He invested in rice and opened the area's first rice mill, but lost the business and all his capital trying to corner the rice market. After that, Joshua Abraham Norton disappeared. He returned a few months later as His Royal Highness, Norton I. He drafted an imperial edict, the first of many, declaring himself emperor and sovereign of the United States and Mexico. The newspapers published it. His reign lasted 21 years; San Francisco was a delighted and willing subject.

He dined in the city's most elegant restaurants and never paid a bill. He regularly rode the cable cars, but never soiled his gloves on a fare box. He was a fastidious man, fussy about his bedecked uniforms which he ordered free, of course, from the finest tailors. He issued his own scrip and paid what debts he chose with that; he watched theatrical performances from the royal boxes. When two stray dogs adopted him, he named them Lazarus and Bummer. They were accorded treatment as princely as his own. When one of the dogs died, its obituary was written and published by Mark Twain, then editor of the Virginia City Territorial Enterprise.

Newspapers regularly published his proclamations and San Francisco nabobs conferred with him on the most serious matters.

He died in 1880 and his empire died with him for he had no heirs; but 30,000 persons attended his funeral. When his remains were moved to a different cemetery in the 1930's, the mayor gave a speech and the municipal band played a concert. Nobody ever found out whether Norton I was a madman or a con man. Nobody cared.

There have been a lot of characters in San Francisco since Norton though none with the old boy's flair. San Franciscans care about their traditional cable cars even more than they do about characters.

San Francisco's first cable car rattled up the Clay Street grade August 2, 1873, its inventor, Andrew Smith Hallidie at the grip. Its detractors had dubbed it "Hallidie's Folly". They were wrong.

Cable cars enjoyed immediate popular and financial success. In a short time, other cable car companies were formed, operating—like Hallidie's—on city franchises. They couldn't lay track and cable fast enough. At the turn of the century, San Francisco was criss-crossed by more than 100 miles of tracks on which more than 400 pieces of rolling stock, from utilitarian postal cars to smarmy black funeral coaches.

Cable cars smoothed San Francisco's hills, prompting a construction boom in areas previously considered impractical.

The cables went into slow decline after the 1906 earthquake; increased operating costs and "practical" methods of transportation, which eventually included the automobile, cut into tariffs and popularity. The city took over operation of the lines in 1912 and the cutbacks in service began. The Clay Street Line, Hallidie's original, shut down, finally, in 1942, despite protests of an enthusiastic, but ineffectual, "Save The Cable Car League". Five years later, then Mayor Roger Lapham suggested that all cable lines be shut down for the good of the city. That kicked off another row which ended in 1955 with a charter provision that cable cars could not be eliminated except by a vote of the people. By the time the fight had ended, only three lines were still in operation, the ones you can ride today.

You don't hear much about Roger Lapham anymore; Mrs. Freda Klussman, the woman who headed the drive to save the cables, is a San Francisco folk hero.

Today, cable car lines carry 13 million people a year in 39 cars over 10 1/2 miles of track—at a substantial financial loss. But the cars and the power house at Washington and Mason Streets are major attractions; the cable car is a National Historic Monument and, excepting the Golden Gate Bridge, the city's most recognizable symbol. There are disadvantages, of course: the cable cars move at only 9 miles per hour; aged equipment tends to malfunction; and automobiles smack into the cars, not to mention the fierce independence of gripmen and conductors.

And there is the bizarre case of a young woman who was aboard a cable car that was involved in an accident in 1964. She sued the city for half a million dollars, claiming the trauma of the incident had turned her into an incurable nymphomaniac. The courts awarded her $50,000.

Another part of San Francisco's tradition is the Victorian house.

Today, they are an endangered species. There will always be a few of these fine old houses around, some well fed on paint, gold leaf and loving care handed down from parent to child; others which have been faithfully restored. But many of them are threatened by a hunt for higher real estate profits, diseases of neglect, snares of progress and loss of territory (which in the case of houses means a shift in the fortunes of the neighborhoods in which they stand). And a few are threatened by their own heritage: they are too large, too intricate or too highly taxed to be maintained.

But the "average" Victorian makes a fine home and one in which you can raise a family; they are roomy, multi-floored and high posted with tiny, hidden gardens in the rear. Who designed the Victorians is anybody's guess. There is a distinct possibility that nobody did. One thing is certain: it was a carpenter's holiday. The bulk of the Victorians were built between 1860 and 1890, mass-produced from redwood and fir.

Hardly any of the people who settled in the new houses, erected in rapidly expanding residential neighborhoods, had ever panned gold in the Sierra or visited a crib in the Barbary Coast. But, they *were* San Franciscans, too. They nailed that extravagant legacy onto the false fronts of their houses, or piled it up on top: Russian-styled cupolas and domes, Turkish spires, spandrels of all shapes, turrets, widow's walks, musician's balconies. The ubiquitous bay window sprouted a variety of forms set off by a cornucopia of the carpenter's art, either individually crafted or ordered from a catalogue ready-made. These houses were not "Victorian," really, they were "San Franciscan": individualistic, frenzied, stately, madcap, interesting, funny, grotesque and diverse as the city in which they were built. They suited the city and its residents and perhaps, by accident, the unique play of light that flits across the San Francisco sky.

In San Francisco, traditional things add a certain character to a unique city and give it style and grace:

Like hospitality. Herb Caen, San Francisco's noted columnist, offered this example recently: when a Gray Line tour bus broke down in the 1100 block of Taylor Street on a cold night, Gene Dockman who runs a coffee shop there reopened his little café and served the shivering tourists hot coffee, doughnuts and pastries—for free. Things like that do happen here. So do other things traditional:

—The insistence by its citizens that San Francisco be called San Francisco, never 'Frisco'.

—The al fresco Sunday luncheons of cold cracked crab, chilled Chablis, sourdough bread, tossed salad.

—The ships in the harbor blowing their whistles at midnight New Year's Eve.

—The wearing of white tie and tails to the annual opening of the Opera.

—The annual Upper Grant Street Fair, the Washington Square Fair, the Columbus Day festivities, the Cherry Blossom Festival, the Beaux Arts Ball, the Castro Street Fair, the blessing of the fleet, the Cinco de Mayo Festival and the art show in Civic Center.

—The start of Christmas shopping the Friday following Thanksgiving.

—The paying of your fare on the cable car when it is crowded and the conductor misses you.

—Sundays spent in Golden Gate Park when autos are banned and the Municipal band plays on and on.

—And never parking in a legal parking space when an illegal one is available.

—Garage sales and flea markets. And fleas.

And to prove the point: if you want to be a real San Franciscan, thumb your nose at Oakland or Los Angeles or New York, any place that isn't San Francisco but has pretensions.

It's tradition.

San Francisco's early
residential areas were
composed of rows of small,
detached houses, many of
them with hidden gardens
and landscaped pathways.
Today (opposite, upper photo)
this can make for remarkable
views of past and present;
this picture was taken at
Alamo Square.

For the nostalgic-minded traveller, four sections of San Francisco are a must:

Mission District: Guerrero Street, from block 800 to block 1500; Dolores Street, from 700 to 1500; Sanchez Street, from 300 to 1700; Noe Street, from 300 to 1600; and 20th, 21st, 22nd and 23rd Streets, from 3000 to 4000.

Pacific Heights: Vallejo Street, from 1600 to 2900; Broadway, from 1700 to 2900; Pacific Avenue, from 1800 to 3500; Jackson Street, from 1100 to 3800; Washington Street, from 2100 to 3900; Pierce Street, from 1900 to 2700; Scott Street, from 1900 to 3000; Divisadero Street, from 1900 to 2700.

Russian Hill: Green Street, from 700 to 1900; Vallejo Street, 1000 block; Russian Hill Place.

Western Addition: Clay Street, from 2400 to 3900; Sacramento Street, from 1100 to 3400; California Street, from 1800 to 3000; Pine Street, from 1800 to 3000; Bush Street, from 1600 to 2900; Sutter Street, from 1400 to 2700; Post Street, from 1300 to 2600; Laguna Street, from 1600 to 3000; Buchanan Street, from 1700 to 2600; Webster Street, from 1700 to 3000; Steiner Street, from 1800 to 3000; Baker Street, from 1400 to 2100.

The San Francisco Farmers Market, owned
and operated by the city, is a virtual agrarian
United Nations used by more than 700 farmers
of almost every nationality. The bounty
varies with the season. Shopping here for
bargains has become a tradition for
thousands of Bay Area residents. But the
market is also a place to visit with old
friends, gossip and exchange views on growing
larger and tastier vegetables.

When on May 10, 1869 the Union Pacific and
the Central Pacific joined the railway lines
at Promontory, Utah, banners in San Francisco
proclaimed: "San Francisco Annexes the
United States." But baseball makes Americans
of us all, even when certain chauvinists
cheer only the San Francisco Giants.

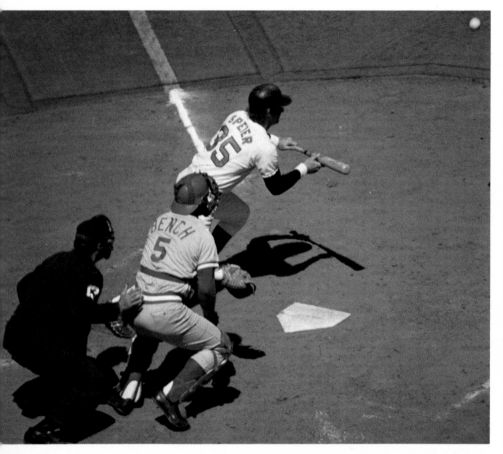

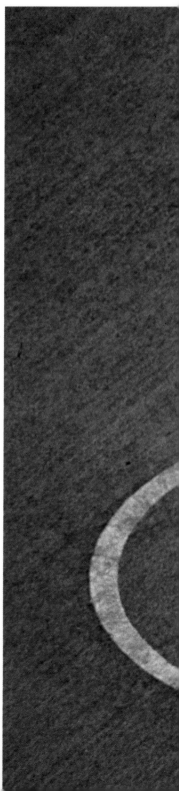

Wine is an inseparable part of the San Francisco scene; much of it is aged in cellars in the Napa Valley such as this one owned by Beringer Brothers.

Little has dimmed the
popularity of the city's
cable cars. Every now
and again someone
makes suggestions
regarding more efficient
modes of transport,
but the resulting clamor
from the public can be
heard around the world.
In 1947 members of a
San Francisco citizen's
committee resolved to "Save
the Cable Cars" and put
the issue on a ballot.
They succeeded.
Now there is a provision
in the city charter
that guarantees
perpetuation of the three
remaining lines.
The San Francisco Municipal
Railway barns at Washington
and Mason Streets, house
the century old power system
that drives the city's cable cars.
In its repair shops and work
bays, a dedicated band of
overall-clad artisans, build,
repair and maintain the hard
working little vehicles and keep
them painted and polished.
The building serves also as a
transit museum, with old cable
cars and other memorabilia;
it is open to the public.

Cable car crewmen are an
adventurous lot, distinct in
their emblazoned berets.
The gripmen who drive the
cars are, like ships' captains,
absolute masters of their
domains, a role which can lead
to altercations with unruly.
passengers or careless
motorists. Once boarding
cable cars at the Powell-Market
turntable was a free-for-all.
The city has now inaugurated
more orderly, if less exciting,
procedures. Because the
turntables are unpowered,
the crews have to reverse the
cars by hand. Passengers
used to help; the practice has
been curbed for safety reasons.

ROOTS AND NEIGHBORS

When San Francisco finally sank its roots, it sank them in the neighborhoods where the people live.

People push the pencils and pay the taxes. They build the bridges and sail the fishing boats. They mow the lawns in the parks and cook the meals in the restaurants. They carry the hods and paint the houses, unload the ships and dig up the streets, drive the cable cars and run the power plants. They bake the bread and make the children and decorate the caskets.

"Lived in this neighborhood all your life?"

"Not yet."

San Francisco has a lot of neighborhoods, some ethnic, some geographic, some economic, or a combination of the three. Many are rarely noticed, like Bret Harte or Corona Heights. Others are just there, like the Richmond (inner and outer). Still others are very famous like Chinatown or North Beach.

The Chinese first arrived in San Francisco about the same time almost everybody else did—during the gold rush. Those that did not head for the gold fields stayed on in the city and worked mainly as domestics. The construction of the Pacific portion of the transcontinental railroad brought thousands and thousands of Chinese into California: or rather, they were shipped in, like cattle, and herded to the construction sites. By the late 1860's there were more than 15,000 Chinese laborers working on the railroad and when the eastern and western lines were linked at Promontory, Utah, they found themselves out of work. Many of them returned to San Francisco and settled. Some became fishermen while others worked as domestics or tradesmen. Still others were shrewd entrepreneurs: by 1871, the Chinese dominated the city's garment and cigar manufacturing industries. Their timing couldn't have been worse.

There was a economic depression in the late 1870's. Money was tight and jobs were scarce. A lot of small businesses went under, while Chinese enterprises prospered. The Chinese became the targets of pent-up frustration and fear. They were humiliated, their businesses looted and burned, their children beaten: legislators passed laws designed solely to harass them. Thus threatened by the white world, the Chinese created a world of their own and walled it off from the rest of San Francisco with their language, mores, dress and laws.

The original Chinatown, built up around Grant Avenue, was destroyed in the 1906 fire: it was rebuilt.

Behind the ornate facades of its grand restaurants, despite the obvious opulence of certain ranking family organizations and business firms, parts of today's Chinatown reflect scenes from the original: there are severe health problems among many of the elderly; there is a lingering stink of decay in some of its back alleys, and there are buildings where 40 persons share the same toilet.

The old walls around Chinatown have crumbled, slowly. There are problems, but Chinatown is no longer isolated from San Francisco.

Near Chinatown, across Broadway where Grant Avenue becomes Upper Grant, and northwesterly along Columbus is the other famous neighborhood, North Beach and its cousin, Little Italy. Sometimes it is hard to tell the two apart. The neighborhood is a conglomeration of apartments, old established Italian businesses, shops, newer boutiques, markets, family-style restaurants serving quantites of hearty, plain fare for reasonable prices. It is filled by aromas of brine and wine and garlic and cheese, a variety of bars (some of them without signs) and dance halls and jazz joints that range from Italian and Irish to gay and grand funk.

Little Italy runs along and off Columbus, in North Beach; it is still a heavily Italian neighborhood, bright, sunny and lively. Even persons who once lived there and moved away often return to shop, gossip and continue old friendships. The Italians have always been identified with San Francisco's fishing industry. Old photographs of the fishing fleet at anchor, when Fisherman's Wharf was situated in the lee of Telegraph Hill at the end of Union Street, show hundreds of lateen, rigged feluccas. The pictures, some of which hang in the San Francisco Maritime Museum, could have been taken on the Mediterranean, save for telltale false-front houses scattered across Telegraph Hill.

Fishing is no longer a major industry, but Italian names still dominate it.

North Beach has been a well-populated area almost from the beginning, numbering among its people all manner of artists and bohemians. But its name was immortalized in the 1950's with the arrival of the so-called Beatniks with their black-clad old ladies, beards, sandals, blank verse and coffee houses.

North Beach's common is Washington Square and its church, the Church of Sts. Peter and Paul which sits at its northern edge. You can find people to talk with here in the square, attend its annual fair and watch the Columbus Day parade.

Between Chinatown and North Beach is Broadway which is not really a neighborhood, but you may see some neighbors there. Broadway is a relatively tame descendant of the late Barbary Coast; you can watch the ladies dancing without any clothes on, but you cannot touch. There are a number of clubs along the strip and you can see a wide variety of activity. There are racy movie houses and racy bars, some of the city's best jazz clubs and, in the immediate area, some of the most exclusive restaurants. There is also Enrico's, one of San Francisco's classiest bistros and one which still pours a full drink at a reasonable price.

Broadway's tinsel-town atmosphere and illusion of sin may be boring, but it is never dull.

Broadway runs east-west nearly the width of the city; its neon section is on the eastern, bay side. At its western end, where it is referred to as Broadway Street, sit some of the most elegant mansions in the West. Wide leafy streets cross and parallel it. Rolls Royces park along its curbs. This is Pacific Heights, a place of understated elegance and great wealth. It is not your average neighborhood. It also tends to be rather tame, while neighborhoods like Chinatown or North Beach, that combine housing with pleasure and business, tend toward the opposite.

Another example in this latter category is Japantown, a neighborhood along Post Street between Fillmore and Octavia. If you have a taste for tempura or sushi or Japanese hardware stores or samurai movies, which a lot of San Franciscans do, that's the place to go. There's even a Korean restaurant and one of the best stands of Victorian houses in the city. There is also the annual Cherry Blossom Festival with its drums and drama.

Well below Japantown, across the western Addition and Market Street, are two more of San Francisco's oldest neighborhoods, the Mission District and South of Market.

South of Market is also called South O' The Slot, the slot being the cable car grip slots that ran up the center of Market Street years ago; the slots divided more than Market Street. They separated the bossing men from the working men, and the working men lived on the south side. They were predominantly Irish, but they were also Swedes, Slavs, Russians, Poles, Hollanders and Germans. They lived in their Victorian houses and drank in the local saloons, ate onions and organized solid, rollicking, old world neighborhoods, South of Market and out along Mission. These were the men and women who literally built the city. San Francisco is a union town and the unions came out of the blood and sweat and courage of those neighborhoods.

The South of Market district was industrial and studded with warehouses; the Mission was primarily residential. That much hasn't changed and there is still a lot of the old Irish earthiness around, too. There are still Irish taverns on Mission Street, squeezed in between the furniture stores and garages and markets, though the area is primarily a Spanish speaking one today, filled with newcomers from Mexico, El Salvador, Nicaragua and Guatemala.

Much of the city's industry is still in the South of Market and Mission neighborhoods; so are most of the city's remaining workingman's saloons like the Transbay Tavern at Fourth and Bryant. The Transbay is run by Al Opatz, a ham-fisted Pole who wears funny hats and regularly buys the house a round of drinks.

Few workingmen at the Transbay today wear overalls. Mostly they are young executives or television crews or writers or recording industry people or engineers from the banks or TV stations and magazines that now keep offices in remodeled warehouses that once held hogsheads and steel.

"It's still a good neighborhood," says Opatz. "Lots of different kinds of people."

That is true of almost every neighborhood in San Francisco; by no means do all the Chinese live in Chinatown nor the Italians in North Beach nor the wealthy in Pacific Heights. This makes diverse and interesting neighborhoods.

One of the busiest and most noted streets in the world, Grant Avenue runs through the center of Chinatown from its southern to its northern boundary.

For many visitors, San Francisco's Chinatown evokes thoughts of mystery and romance: a fascinating glimpse of the Orient transplanted. Even San Franciscans view it as a neighborhood of special sights and sounds with distinct architecture and a profitable flair for the dramatic. At left, *the local offices of the Bank of Canton. Right, an old woman rests a moment in a Chinatown doorway; a clerk in the Chinatown branch of the U.S. Post Office stamps an outgoing parcel.*

Chinatown at work and play:
Upper left, *an elderly
gentleman in Portsmouth
Square contemplates his next
move in a game of Jok Kay,
a Chinese version of chess;*
lower left, *a member of the
drum and bugle corps of
Saint Mary's Catholic Chinese
Center pratices in traditional
costume;* lower right, *a girl
performs a move of the Tai
Chi Chuan, a Taoist exercise.*
Right, *a tot goes marketing
with grandmother on Stockton
Street.*

The Chinese community
of San Francisco is one of
the largest in the Western
world: well over a 100,000
people. It concentrates on
Bush Street, Powell Street,
Broadway and Kearny
Street and it has built the
largest Buddhist temple
in the United States.
The history of the Chinese
people on the Western coast
can be traced in the Chinese
Historical Museum.

The Chinese have undertaken all sorts of trades and occupations in San Francisco, contributing to the charm of the city with their customs and art.

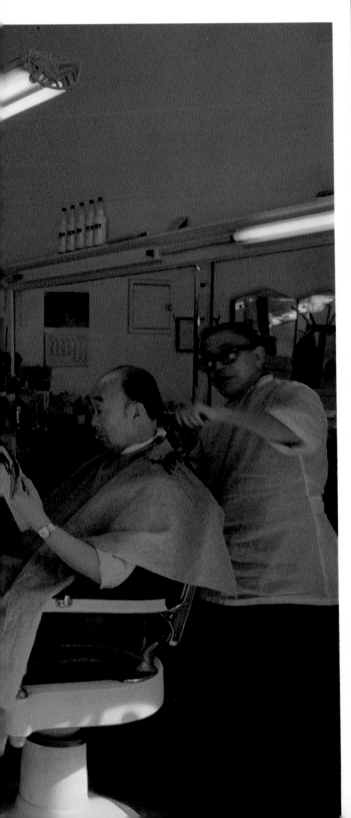

In the center of North Beach is Washington Square: neighborhood park, fairgrounds, a place to dance and a spot to doze. At its northern edge is the Church of Sts. Peter and Paul, which serves the area's Italian, Roman Catholic community. North Beach with adjacent Little Italy is a solid, old-world neighborhood; it is also home to many of the city's writers, artists and bohemians.

Little Italy, the heart of San Francisco's Italian community, abounds with traditional hospitality and cuisine. Its musicians are legion and its bocceball courts ever popular. In its out-of-the-way cafes, old friends can share a game of cards or reminisce over a glass of wine or bitters. The Italians have long been a part of the San Francisco community and have placed upon it their own, unmistakable stamp of humor and informality.

When the Italians first arrived in San Francisco, it was "per fare l'America", "to make their America", to make a new life. Now they form a hard-working lively community, still in touch with their native Italian "paese", their little village, and the results of their favorite Italian soccer team. They have added their local dishes to the San Francisco cuisine, which also boasts the finest European-style loaf in America. North Beach merchants and businesses provide staples catering to the neighborhood's primarily Italian palate.

*The Upper Grant Street Fair
is one of the city's most
popular annual events.
It highlights the works and
handicrafts of area artists
and artisans. Several of the
neighborhood's bohemians
who always attend the fair
are works of art themselves.*

Broadway is a tame descendant of the old Barbary Coast and does its best, with bars and topless joints, to carry on the old wickedness of the 1850's.

Nihonmachi means Japan Town, a complex multiblock area that furthers Japanese customs and trade in San Francisco.
Pagodas, restaurants, flowershops- the Japanese community has added its Oriental grace to the city.

Perhaps the most colorful of the city's celebrations, the Cherry Blossom Festival is sponsored annually by San Francisco's Japanese community.

San Francisco's Historic Mission Dolores was founded in 1776 by Fr. Francisco Palou, a member of the Spanish expeditionary force that built the original colony of Yerba Buena. The mission, at Dolores and 16th Streets, still serves the neighborhood's Roman Catholic community. The San Francisco mission was one of a string of 21 missions, begun in 1769, along the California coast from San Diego in the south to Sonoma in the north.

THE EDGE OF THE BAY

There has been a long and friendly disagreement over just who opened the first restaurant on Fisherman's Wharf, and when. No one really seems to remember—perhaps on purpose for the sake of prolonging the discussion.

But it is a fact that right after the First World War, a lot of San Franciscans discovered what a lot of fishermen and fishermen's wives in North Beach had known all along: if you wanted fresh fish or shellfish, you just went down to the dock and bought it off the boat. Or you could eat fresh fish, just cooked, at one of the little restaurants suddenly popping up along Fisherman's Wharf.

As more and more people flocked to the area, restauranteurs set up black cauldrons in front of their establishments. In crab season, they cooked the catch before their customer's eyes, to be taken home or eaten at the restaurants. San Franciscans had never seen the likes of it before: competition for the diner's dollar became fierce. Barkers attracted the potentially hungry inside the eating establishments much the same way barkers today lure the potentially thirsty inside Broadway's topless bars.

The Wharf in those days was where it is today, at the foot of Taylor Street. It had been moved from its original site at the eastern end of Union Street in 1900, when the State of California took over management of the port.

The fish "rush", really boomed during World War II when the city's and the Bay Area's population exploded. After that it was all over for the once quaint little quay. A quay where you could watch the Italian fisherfolk mending their nets and singing, where you could buy fish off the boat; where you could find a parking space on a Saturday; where a pair of young San Francisco lovers could spend a long evening together over dinner and a bottle of wine in the corner booth of some joint—without a reservation or a 90-minute wait—and the patron knew them by name. The rush is still on at Fisherman's Wharf, though the fish have all but been lost along the way.

It is easy, even today, to hang over the rail of the anchorage where the small fishing fleet ties up and feel the pull and romance of the sea; the feeling leaves when you turn around. The neon lights, fast food joints, gimcrack shops and other "commercial" enterprises are about as nautical or nostalgic as a carnival midway. Still, the Wharf is one of the top attractions in San Francisco. But whatever it has become, it is now beyond the control of those San Franciscans who preferred it as it was. It is quite simple: Fisherman's Wharf changed because it was too successful.

The irony in all this, for San Francisco traditionalists, lies just down the street from the Wharf: The Cannery, and a bit further, Ghirardelli Square. The Cannery was once a real cannery and the Square a woolen mill and later a chocolate factory. The original buildings have been preserved intact; within their walls are theaters and restaurants, a variety of shops and boutiques, trees and fountains and a lot of nostalgia. The owners took a chance, deciding you can preserve heritage and still run a profitable business. They were right.

This is an area where San Francisco's heritage endured, Aquatic Park, the San Francisco Maritime Museum, the Hyde Street Pier with its historic old ships riding at anchor (and open to the public): there is the picturesque "Buena Vista" café where Irish Coffee was born and Victoria Park with its cable car turn-table.

As you move west along the edge of the bay away from the Fisherman's Wharf area, you end up in the Marina district with its very busy bayside park, known as Marina Green, and the fashionable, Mediterranean-style houses with their huge picture windows looking out over the bay and the Golden Gate Bridge and the dramatic Marin County headlands.

Further along the coastline are San Francisco's two old soldiers, The Presidio and Fort Point.

Sometimes, on a foggy afternoon, walking through the Presidio's forests, it is difficult to keep in mind that this place is an active military post, headquarters for the United States Sixth Army, and a military reserve since Col. Juan Bautista de Anza started building the first fort there in 1776. The Presidio is not unware of its history; its Officers Mess, claimed to be the oldest building in the city, incorporates within its walls part of the original de Anza fort. Within the Presidio compound which is open to the public, is the national cemetery with its rows of small white headstones, a silent accounting of the cost of war.

Old Fort Point, on the other hand, never went to war. Today, it sits squat and disarmed under an arch of the Golden Gate bridge especially designed to accommodate it. It is an historic museum and the only fort in the west built along the classic lines of fortifications of the 1850's. Once it mounted 127 cannon to protect the Golden Gate and the city from all enemies. The enemies never came; Fort Point never fired a hostile shot. Neglected for years, Fort Point has been restored and is open to the public. Its breakwater provides footing for anglers and a perfect spot to see the underpinnings of the great bridge which soars above it.

There are a lot of words that can describe the Golden Gate Bridge; they have all been used. And there are a lot of spots from which to take photographs of it. They have all been discovered. On the day the bridge opened, May 27, 1937, more than 200,000 persons walked across it. When it opened for motorized traffic, the following day, 25,000–plus vehicles used it.

Since that opening day, thousands of people have walked across the bridge every year, auto traffic has exceeded the bridge's capacity to move it smoothly and without delay from one shore to the other, and more than 500 despairing souls have jumped off it to their deaths despite continuing efforts to curb that practice.

It is San Francisco's landmark, a great soaring suspension bridge with a span of 4,200 feet (1,280 meters) making it one of the very longest in the world. The huge bridge was "built" by a pint-sized man named Joseph B. Strauss who saw it as a rainbow in steel and a tribute to man's endurance.

South of the bridge on the city's Pacific rim on the Point Lobos head-lands, Lincoln Park lies green and gentle. The park features a golf course on lands once used to bury the city's paupers. The park is also the site of the stately Palace of the Legion of Honor, a gift to San Francisco from Adolph Spreckles and his wife Alma de Bretteville, honoring the dead of World War I. The Palace is the repository for a large collection of works of art, much of it by Rodin. His most recognizable piece, "The Thinker", broods eternally in the museum's atrium.

From the headlands, the coast runs south to the sea and Ocean Beach where the Pacific Ocean rolls endlessly against San Francisco's shore. The winds which perpetually cool the city streak in over the breakers, bending the cyprus trees which form a green and living oceanfront wall for Golden Gate Park.

Golden Gate Park is the great natural wonder of the city entirely created by man. Narcissism aside, there is no other park quite like it anywhere. There is very little the park does not have and first and foremost is acres of civilized wilderness, green and ringed with solitude. But there are also museums, an academy of science, lakes, boating facilities, bicycle paths, fly-casting pools, soccer fields, lawn bowling greens, tennis courts, windmills, a polo field, the Japanese Tea Garden, the band shell and Sunday concerts.

Where the park now stands was once only sand, clay and little else. In the 1860's, the city fathers decided San Francisco should have a park system, a decision made by many American cities in those years which grew out of the preservation theories of planner Frederick Law Olmstead, Sr. City officials consulted the great man himself (while he was designing the campus at the University of California at Berkeley) and while most of his suggestions were eventually ignored, his concepts were not. Golden Gate Park was the most impressive result.

It was designed and begun by a young engineer named William Hall and the park today is much as he envisioned it. It was Hall who discovered how to plant the sand and hold the topsoil: a discovery made when, on a survey mission, he dropped his horse's feedbag containing barley. He scooped the mess back into the bag but the horse refused to eat the sandy meal. Hall tossed it all out in disgust. When he returned to the site weeks later, he found the barley had sprouted.

Men planted barley and then trees and shrubs. Even the rocks and cliffs, most of them anyway, were hand crafted.

Hall ran a foul of politicians and finally quit his job in disgust. His successor in 1889 was a Scots gardener named John McLaren. It was McLaren who built the park, fought off intruders, hid the statues erected at City Hall insistence behind bushes and reigned over the park as a benevolent despot until he died in 1943. He wanted the park to be a park.

San Franciscans have adopted his philosophy: today even a modest proposal for a new building in the park is cause for general mutiny.

Out in San Francisco Bay, 1½ miles
north of Fisherman's Wharf, lies a 12 acre
island of solid rock known as Alcatraz.
It became a federal penitentiary in 1934
and it has housed such notorious gangsters
as Al Capone and "Machine Gun" Kelly.
The name was given to it by Juan Manuel de
Ayala, supposedly because of the flock of pelicans
nesting there (Alcatraz means pelican in
Spanish).

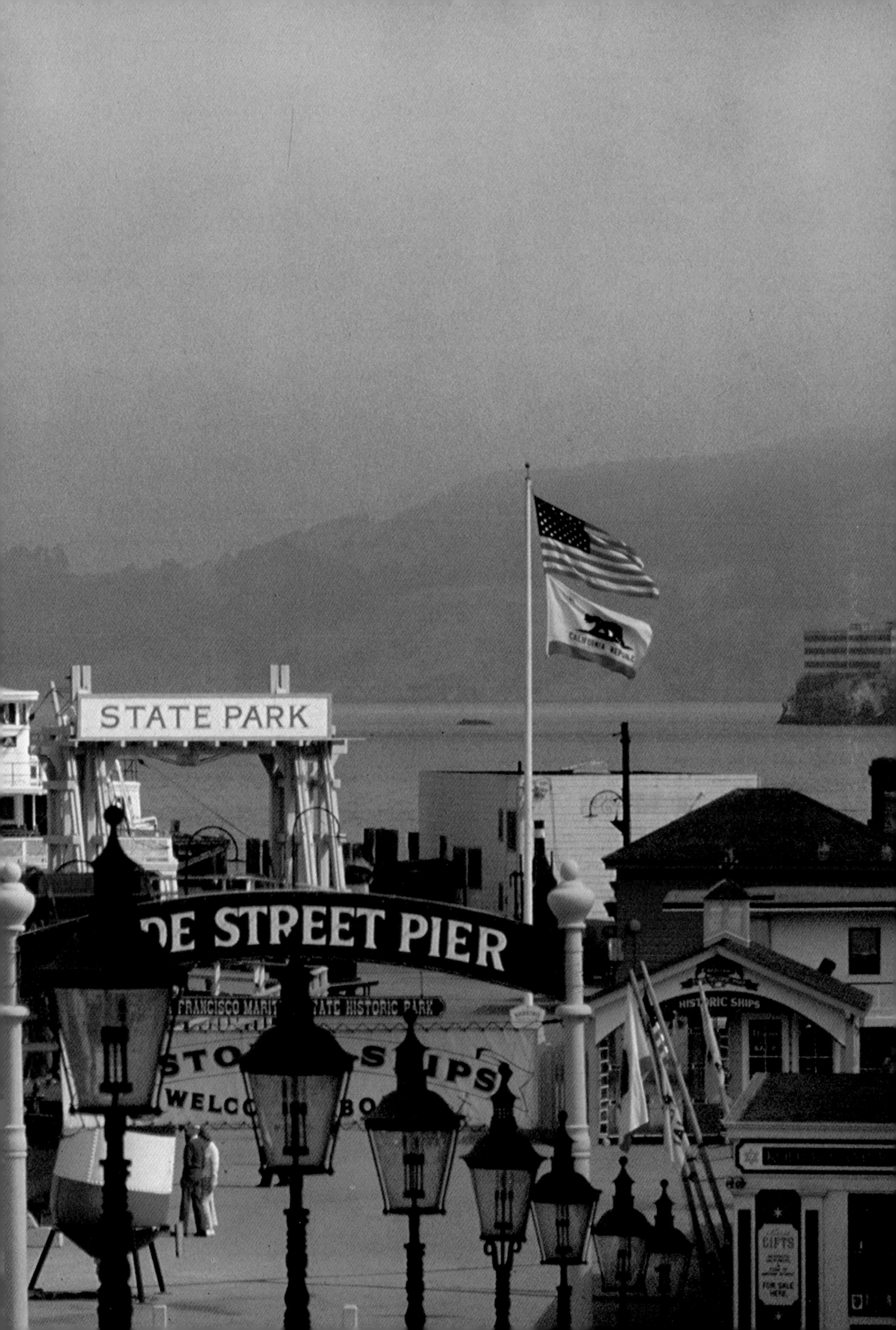
STATE PARK
DE STREET PIER
HISTORIC SHIPS
GIFTS

At the western edge of Fisherman's Wharf, Aquatic Park and the Hyde Street Pier, a state park, provide glimpses of San Francisco's past. The pier serves as a museum for several old, historic ships including a lumber schooner and a retired San Francisco ferry boat. The ships are open to the public. The area also has a cable car turn-table and old factories converted into shopping and dining complexes. Even the illumination is from a different era as these gas lamps marching up Hyde Street indicate.

San Francisco's small fishing fleet still carries on a century of tradition, wrestling nature's bounty from the sea.

Once upon a time, The Cannery was a cannery and when it had chopped its last fish, its owners closed the doors and sold out. The new owner, a man named Leonard Martin, converted it into a colorful complex of restaurants, shops and boutiques. Like its nearby competitor, Ghirardelli Square, once a woolen mill and later a chocolate factory, something of San Francisco's past was preserved to delight its present residents and visitors. Both complexes are situated near Aquatic Park and Fisherman's Wharf.

Memorial Day at the Presidio's national cemetery is always a somber occasion. Five generations of soldiers lie buried here, many of them very young when they died. Homage is paid once a year to memories of glories past.

Old Fort Point, under the Golden Gate Bridge was the last of three forts built on the site. Erected in the early 1850's, it mounted 127 cannon to guard the entrance of the bay. No enemy ships ever came within their sights.

Surfers, fishermen, seagulls, commuters and the fog all see the Golden Gate Bridge from a slightly different perspective.

Lincoln Park attracts the athlete and the aesthete: golf for the former and for the latter, the Palace of the Legion of Honor with its large collection of Rodins and other art works.

San Francisco's western edge
is a favorite place for
swimmers, above on the Seal
Rock wildlife sanctuary a few
yards offshore, and joggers,
below, on Ocean Beach along
the ocean's edge.

The Children's Zoo is one of the most popular sections of the San Francisco Zoological Gardens, where youngsters can feed and pat the tame animals, such as sheep, pigs, llamas. An occasional daring squirrel might also be met on the sunny paths.

Man and nature in harmony:
Fleishhacker Zoo
(pages 142-143) *and Golden*
Gate Park.

Golden Gate Park's famed Japanese Tea Garden offers visitors space for refreshment and reflection along its flowered, curving walkways.

Golden Gate Park has
something for almost everyone:
the Steinhart Aquarium, the
De Young Museum, Sunday
concerts and sports, nature
and kinship.

*It was a Scotsman, John McLaren, who in 1887 took over
as manager of Golden Gate Park and transformed the sand
dunes into the gardens we see today. The Park is a man-made
wonder. The gingerbread flower conservatory —a humid,
tropical wonderland —was manufactured in New York
and its parts shipped around Cape Horn in crates.*

UNCAPTURED SAN FRANCISCO

No book conveys the truly subtle sweetness of life in San Francisco. Uncaptured, for example, is the salt smell of a summer mist or the heady aroma of cappucino spilling into a cold, rainy winter's eve from the old Tosca cafe on Columbus; the precise tone of South of Market's bawdy wit or the midnight wail of an ambulance in Eureka Valley; and that exact moment when the first drop of winter rain arrives or the last wisp of summer fog vanishes.

There is another intangible: another earthquake, 1906-style, is on the way, perhaps today or next week or next year. Most San Franciscans deal with it by not dealing with it at all. There is little advertisement of the fact that if you are a San Franciscan you are sitting on Mother Nature's time-bomb. And it's ticking.

To realistically appreciate San Francisco, one must view it in this way: what is here today may be gone tomorrow. That does not apply solely to earthquakes. San Francisco is also a city in transition, and, if you will, a success: but this very success threatens to be more destructive than any upheaval of nature.

At night the twinkling towers of the financial district and the shining, multi-storied and profitable apartment towers that have replaced older, smaller and not so profitable apartment houses look exciting and contemporary. Viewed in another light these buildings are a steel glass army laying waste a city that made architectural intimacy a way of life.

Allan Jacobs, the city's planning director from 1967 to 1974 when the city's skyline was rising as fast as its tax rate, once observed with some frustration, "As beautiful as San Francisco is, we can only chip away' at that beauty so much. If we do not proceed wisely and carefully, someday... San Francisco won't be there."

Preservation is not necessarily profitable, nor great, natural beauty inviolate. But if there is a way to make them so, San Franciscans will discover how and share it with all who come to the great city by the bay where dreams and hope never die.

The first edition of SAN FRANCISCO
was published in January 1976 by
les éditions du pacifique, Papeete, Tahiti
in cooperation with and for **European book
Company** San Francisco.
The book was planned and the photos were
taken by Bernard Hermann. The text
was written by Scott Blakey.